How to Play Pool – Guide

Table of Contents

Introduction

Billiards (or cue sports) is a term for a lot of different games which generally include the use of a cue stick, billiard balls, and a billiards table. The sport itself has evolved into a lot of different sports and activities with different rules and regulations and it's safe to say that playing and mastering every variation of the game is fairly difficult and challenging. In order to have a better understanding of the wide variety of games included in the term "billiards", there exists a division of three major types of games which are played using similar equipment:

- Pool is definitely the most famous and widely played variation of billiards and it is also known as pocket billiards in North America. Pool is played both casually and professionally since pool tables can be found both in billiards clubs and regular bars. What makes is distinct in the family of cue sports is the fact that it's played on a table with six pockets (holes) and the table is somewhat smaller than the one used for other billiards games. The decision does not stop here since there are hundreds of different pool games. The most famous ones include nine-ball, eight-ball, straight pool. Pool is the most beginner-friendly variation and the book is going to focus on this variation the most. The usual goal is to pocket all of your balls before your opponent.

Standard pool equipment

- Snooker is a completely different variation of billiards as it's played on a much larger table (approximately 12 feet by 6 feet) and it's played with a significantly larger amount of cue balls than pool since pool is played with 8 or 9 balls and snooker is played with 22 balls. The game consists of hitting the balls in correct order and scoring more points than your opponent. Because of its overall complexness and the amount of skill needed, snooker is a sport mostly enjoyed by professionals and there are a lot of famous tournaments.

A professional snooker match

- Carom billiards is probably the least famous type of cue sports and it has never reached the popularity of pool and billiards. It's played on a table without pockets with dimensions of 5 feet by 10 feet. Scoring points is called caroming and it includes hitting both the opponent's ball and the target ball. The origin of this sport is not well-known but historians think the sport belongs to 18th century France. The sport is rarely played casually or professionally in the Western world.

A carom billiards table with no pockets

Pool is definitely the most beginner-friendly billiards discipline and everyone looking to start playing should start with pool. Snooker is more complex and that is why it gets recognition by professionals. Snooker should also be included in the 2020 Olympic Games following its recognition by the International Olympic Committee (IOC).

Brief History

One should know that each billiards sport derived from outdoor activities which included a stick and a ball. These games are usually referred to as *ground billiards* because they were played on the ground and resembled golf, croquet, and modern billiards. The early beginning of billiards is usually associated with 14th and 15th century France.

Ground billiards

It was the kings of France who helped make billiards famous and who finally made way for modern-looking billiards into the life of aristocrats. Before this era, there were no tables for sports and games similar to billiards and it was Louis XI who owned the first table for billiards. Following leaders of France kept the tradition and Louis XIV made it more and more popular, creating a clear division of ground-based similar sports such as golf and croquet and table billiards.

Funny enough, carom billiards was the first cue sport which hit it big and became popular on the market. However, it reached its peak of popularity in countries outside of the Western world and its fame became to decline over the last couple of decades because of its lack of innovation. After carom billiards became popular, different obstacles and traps were used to make the game more interesting and it's funny to see how holes were essentially invented as obstacles and should have been avoided during a match. However, they later became targets which led to the development of different games such as pool and its derivations and snooker.

Pool was generally a term which referred to betting and a lot of sports which were not connected to cue sports were referred to as pool sports as they involved betting. However, the term eventually became attached only to this specific type of billiards and pool reached its prime level of fame in the late 19th century or the beginning of the 20th century. Annual tournaments were held all around the world and people were going crazy about the sport but it eventually collapsed around 1950's mostly because of the World War II.

The release of "The Hustler", a movie about a pool player who was portrayed by Paul Newman, is considered to be the point where pool and billiards sports started rising to fame again and it's the movie we should thank for keeping the sport popular up until the current day.

Paul Newman in the movie "The Hustler"

Snooker developed as a billiards game in the late 19th century by certain British Army officers which came up with a game which mixed the rules of several other variations of the sports in order to come up with a sport played with 15 red balls and one black ball. However, it was Sir Neville Chamberlain who set the foundation for the game by finalizing its set of rules and regulations.

The reason why billiards sports are so popular around the world is the fact that British Army was controlling a large chunk of the colony world and they spread their ideas outside the Western world.

Equipment

Pool definitely can't be enjoyed without proper equipment and it belongs to a group of sports whose equipment can't be easily replaced by an alternative. What you need to properly enjoy a game of pool is a table, balls, and cue sticks.

Pool tables are usually smaller than snooker tables, for instance, and there are various approved dimensions. They are usually called by their length and the approved dimensions include a 9-foot table, 8.5 ft, 8 ft, and 7ft. The reason they are referred to by their length is that the length to width ratio is always 2:1. This means that the 8-foot table always has the width of 4 ft, etc.

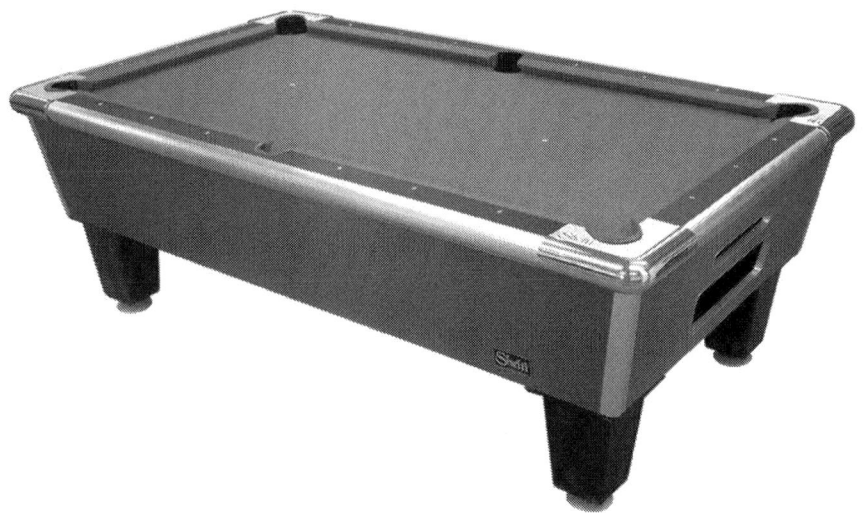

A regular pool table

The table has six holes or pockets and it's in the shape of a perfect rectangle. Pockets are placed in each corner and in the middle of longer sides, dividing the table into two perfect squares.

The pockets sometimes feature a bag which simply captures any balls that fall through and sometimes there is a tunnel which takes the balls to the same place and displays them in the order they were pocketed.

Balls used to play pool slightly differ from balls used for other cue sports. They are larger than balls used for snooker but they are significantly smaller than ones used for carom. The standard allowed weight ranges from 5.5 to 6 oz and the allowed size is around 2.25 in or 57 mm with a small margin of allowed error. The number of balls used varies from game to game but there are 15 numbered balls and their order is predetermined.

They are divided into two types: solids and stripes. Solids are balls numbered from 1 to 7 and they consist of a single color. Stripes are numbered from 9 to 15 and they consist of the same order of colors as solids but striped with white color. The 8th ball is black and it's used as the final ball in eight-ball game.

Pool balls arranged legally with a white, cue ball next to them

The cue ball is white and it is either larger or has a magnet in the middle the internal mechanism can recognize it and return it where it can be removed easily. This type of mechanism is mostly used for coin-operated tables since you shouldn't have access to other balls once you pocket them.

Cue sticks used to play pool are usually 1.5 meters or 59 inches long and they can be made out of numerous different materials such as fiberglass, rock maple, different types of wood, aluminum, etc. The normal weight of a cue stick ranges between 17 and 21 ounces with the 19oz sticks being the most popular. The tip is no more than 14 mm in diameter which is precise and sufficient enough for this sport in particular. Different sports use different types and sizes of cue sticks and playing with a stick which was not intended to be used for pool, in particular, may result in a decreased performance.

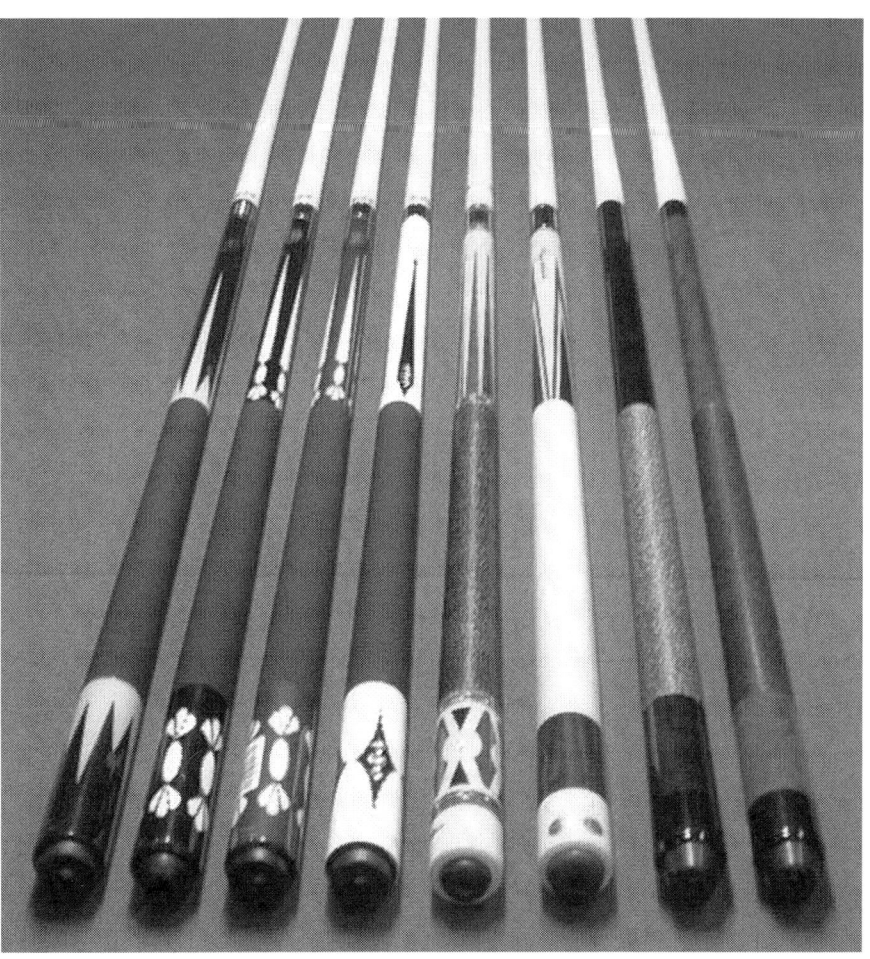

Cue sticks

Different Variations of the Game with Rules

There are a lot of different games you can play on the pool table and you should immediately know that you can't really play snooker table games on a pool table efficiently. That being said, the eBook will focus on games played on the pool table considering the fact that this table and these games are the most beginner-friendly. The most famous pool games include eight-ball, nine-ball, and one-pocket.

Eight-ball

Eight-ball is a variation of pool table games which has become so popular that the game itself is often referred to as "pool" or "billiards" in certain countries, even though it's incorrect. The game is played with fifteen balls excluding the white cue ball. The rules are quite simple and that is what made the game so popular with beginners.

The game starts by arranging the balls in a rack shaped like a triangle in a random order with the 8th ball being in the middle. One of the players proceeds to hit the ball and at least 4 balls should hit the cushions (sides) or one of them should be pocketed if the shot is to be declared legal. If the breaker pockets only the 8 ball while breaking, he has automatically won the game. After the breaking, players take turns only when a foul is committed of when a player fails to pocket their target ball. One player is assigned to solids (balls 1-7) and another player is assigned to stripes (9-15) according to the first ball the first player pockets. This excludes the break shot.

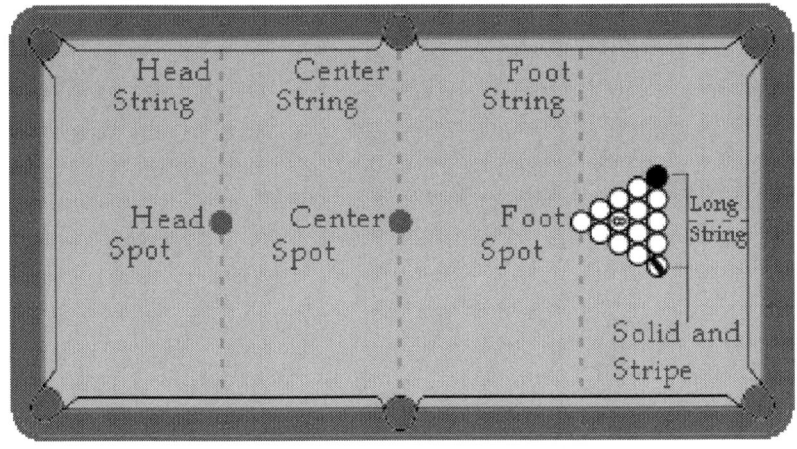

A figure of a pool table with the proper arrangement of the balls for a break shot

The game is won after one of the players pockets the 8 ball. The 8 ball may only be pocketed after the player has successfully got rid of all of their balls by pocketing them. The 8 ball may only be pocketed in the designated hole and that hole can be chosen by the player or determined by the last player's pocketed ball. The game is also won if the opponent pockets the 8 ball before his other target balls or if the 8 ball is pocketed in the wrong hole. Even if the eight ball is pocketed in the right hole but the player commits a foul, the opposing player wins the match.

There are many fouls which can be committed and get to know them all can be quite difficult. However, there are ones you simply must avoid. Let's take a look at some of them.

- Touching the opponent's balls or the 8 ball before striking your own.

- No ball comes touches the cushions or is pocketed after you strike the cue ball and hit your target ball.

- If the cue ball does not touch any ball, a foul is called and the opponent gets to choose where to put the cue ball (ball in hand).

- Moving or touching any of the balls with anything other than the tip of the cue stick.

- Taking your shot before other balls seize to move.

Nine-ball

Nine-ball is the number one choice when it comes to professional matches and tournaments because of its greater complexity over eight-ball. The sport's early beginning can be traced to the 20's in the United States of America. The reason is it the most played professional pool table game is because of its greater complexity but also because matches don't last long and are suitable to be portrayed live on television.

Nine-ball is played on the same table as eight-ball but, this time, only nine of the colored balls are used and those are usually the solids numbered from 1 to 9. The goal of the game is to hit the lowest numbered ball on the table and pocket the 9 ball before your opponent. Contrary to eight-ball pool, players don't need to pocket all balls before pocketing the 9 ball but they do always have to hit the lowest numbered ball on the table.

Balls are arranged in a diamond formation, starting out with 1 ball on the front end and the 9 ball in the center. Other balls are usually arranged in a random order. A player who breaks the balls needs to aim at the 1 ball since it is currently the lowest numbered ball on the table. If he is able to pocket a ball his turn continues and he still aims for the lowest ball. However, if he makes a foul, for example, when none of the balls hit the cushions, the opposing player can demand another break with him being the new breaker or he can continue as if a regular foul has been committed. If the breaker hits the 1 ball during the break shot and he pockets only the 9 ball, he is declared winner.

A proper rack with the 1 ball in the front and the 9 ball in the middle

During a game of nine-ball, the order of pocketed balls does not matter and any player can pocket the 9 ball and win at any point in the game, as long as the cue ball's first contact is with the lowest numbered ball on the table. Another way to win is if your opponent commits three fouls in a row but only if he is warned after the second one.

There is a special move called the push-out and it occurs after the break shot if one of the players calls for it. The player who performs the break shot can ask for it if he pocketed a ball and the opponent can ask for it if no balls have been pocketed. The push-out means that the person who called for it makes his opponent hit the cue ball in any direction with no real boundaries. Any pocketed balls remain in pockets except the 9 ball which is taken out. After the player performs the push-out, the player who called for it can either take the turn and start playing, or he can let his opponent take the turn. That is why push-outs are often well thought of because doing it badly leaves your opponent with a strong advantage. The perfect shot will make your opponent accept the state and take the turn but the shot will actually be quite difficult to make.

Many different variations of the game derived from nine-ball such as six-ball, seven-ball, but the variation which attracted the most attention is ten-ball because players need to call every ball before pocketing it and the ten-ball simply can't be pocketed during the break shot. People want this game to replace nine-ball as the number one professional pool game but there are already a lot of ten-ball tournaments being held around the world.

One-pocket

One-pocket is yet another pool table game but it's somewhat different than the first two entries on our list. The game is played by two players and the game is different from others because only two pockets are used to pocket balls and those are the corner pockets on the foot side of the table (where the balls are placed before the break shot).

Each player tries to pocket balls to his own pocket before his opponent and the first player to pocket eight balls wins the game. Even though only two pockets are used, players can still put balls in other pockets without committing a foul, even if they put the ball in the opponents pocket but both of these scenarios result in losing your turn and the latter gives your opponent a point.

The break shot is pretty much the same as with other sports but there is no required order of balls in the triangle rack. A legal break shot must consist of at least one pocket ball touching the cushions or being pocketed in any hole. A player who breaks the balls chooses his pocket and he can continue playing as long as he pockets balls in his designated pocket. He can also continue playing if he pockets a ball in the wrong pocket but another ball enters the right one. There are no ties.

Playing one pocket requires a good strategy and a lot of precision

Fouls in the game of one-pocket are usually related to illegal shots or moving the cue ball in an illegal manner such as touching it with anything other than the tip of the cue stick, disturbing other balls while playing the cue ball during the ball-in-hand situations, etc. Balls which are pocketed as a result of a foul are spotted, as well as balls pocketed in any pocket other than the two target ones. Spotting involves putting the balls on the foot spot or somewhere directly behind the foot spot while keeping them stuck to other balls in that area.

One-pocket is played a lot by gamblers even though the game does not involve a lot of luck. Various games derived from one-pocket and the most famous one is called bank pool. Bank pool is somewhat more complex because it requires the player to call every ball and every pocket and the rules do not allow the player to touch anything else other than the ball and the designated pocket.

Snooker

Snooker is not a pool game and it's not played on the same table as other pool games. However, it is one of the most popular cue sports and it's a major choice of sport by professionals. It originated in India in the 19th century and it was the British officers stationed who made the game popular. The first World Snooker Championship was held in 1927 and its popularity is on the rise ever since with professional players earning millions of dollars.

The game is played with a total of 22 balls. There are fifteen red balls racked up at the beginning of the game and they are placed at the foot of the table. There are six colored balls (other than red) and they are placed according to the figure below. The size of a snooker table was set by the World Professional Billiards and Snooker Association and it measures 11 feet 8 inches (357 cm) by 5 feet 10 inches (177.8 cm). There are smaller snooker tables you can see at bars or in homes and their dimensions are approximately 10 feet by 5 feet.

The goal is to use your turn to pocket a red ball in any pocket which awards the player with a point. After pocketing a red ball, the player must pocket a "color" which also awards him with points as follows: yellow – two points, green – three points, brown – four points, blue – five points, pink – six points and black – seven points. After pocketing a color, the player must again pocket a red ball and so on. Pocketed colored balls are returned to their original position shown in the figure. The turn is passed when the player fails to pocket the correct ball. A player must at least touch a red ball or a color in order to avoid a foul. A foul also gives the turn to your opponent and awards him with points.

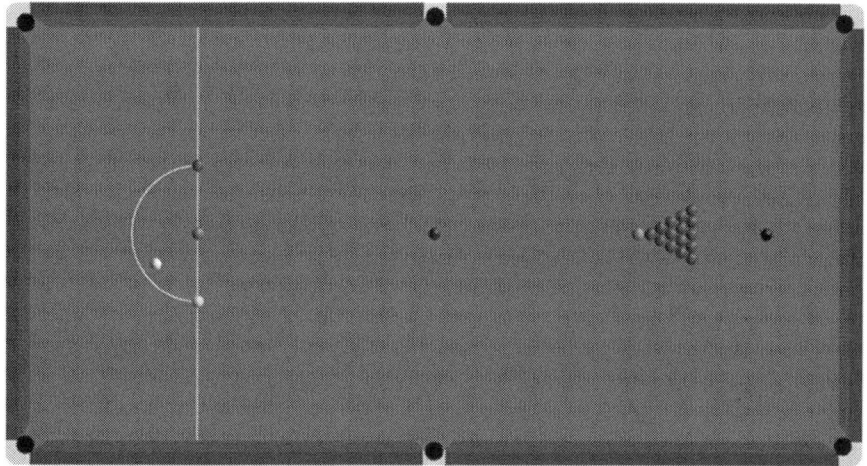

The order of red and the "colored" balls on the table

After all of the red balls have been pocketed, players must pocket the colored balls in the correct order and they are awarded the same amount of points as we mentioned. The order goes like: yellow, green, brown, blue, pink, and black. The player with the most points wins. If both players have the same amount of points after the black ball has been pocketed, the black ball is returned to do a tiebreak.

A break is a term for a consecutive number of points a player earns during his turn. For example, if he pockets three red balls along with a black ball and a yellow ball, his break count would be 12. The break ends when a player fails to pocket his target ball or when he commits a foul. Points gained through the opponent's fouls don't count in the break. The maximum possible break is 155 but it involves the opponent committing a foul beforehand. The maximum traditional break is 147 points and it involves pocketing 15 red balls paired with pocketing the black ball fifteen times and then hitting all of the colors in order. A frame is a term for a single game of snooker and many frames form a match.

Strengthen Your Game

Posture

Even after learning about the rules and even after they play a couple of casual games, most beginners never learn about the correct posture in pool. Most of them align their heads with the wanted path between the cue ball and the object ball which results in a misalignment because, even though your head and your body are aligned with the shot, your hands are not and everything gets interrupted when you kneel to take a shot.

The perfect stance is rather simple yet it yields overwhelmingly positive results.

First of all, line up the stick with the required shot while standing in a normal position and your body will remain on the opposite side of the stick and your dominant hand.

After that, take a step forward with the foot opposite to your dominant arm while bending down and making sure your head stays in the same position as it was while you were standing. This will ensure that the head remains in a natural position which won't feel painful or uncomfortable.

A professional pool player's posture

Finally, you can adjust your head above the line of the shot without causing any pain and score most of your shots. You can either make an open or a closed "bridge" with your non-shooting hand but beginners should definitely learn the open bridge first. Your hand which is not holding the stick should lay around 7 inches (17.5 cm) from the cue ball and you should form an open bridge by spreading your fingers and placing the stick between the index finger and the thumb. Slide it a couple of times to make sure you get the accuracy right before every shot.

Hitting the Ball – Types of Different Shots

Beginners generally don't know about different shots in pool and they are often surprised after they hit the cue ball and it behaves differently than expected. That is because they only know how a regular shot with no spin behaves. That is good for a start but knowing how the spin the ball will give you the edge and enable you to set your position for the next shot or even make it harder for the opponent. However, starting from the basics is the most important part.

A straight shot is a shot which requires you to hit the target ball dead center if you want to pocket and situations in a real match where a straight shot is presented are quite rare. However, mastering the straight shot first will make you more confident and trained for the next type. Start by placing the ball near the pocket and placing the cue ball in the same shot line. Try various shots from various locations by increasing the shot length before you realize you are able to pocket all of them without much thinking.

A straight shot requires hitting the target ball dead center

Angled Shot — when the target ball is near or if the path towards it is clear, you should be able to clearly visualize the path it must take to enter the pocket. The first type of shots included placing the ball on that same line behind the target ball where we had to hit the ball in the center. However, those shots rarely occur in the real game of pool and mastering angled shots is the most important aspect. Shooting an angled shot means placing the cue ball anywhere outside the imagined shot line.

You have to think how the ball is going to deflect after colliding with the cue ball and you definitely need to develop your own rhythm and feeling which require a lot more practice than a regular straight shot. Imagining the ball's path is vital as well as some basic math knowledge.

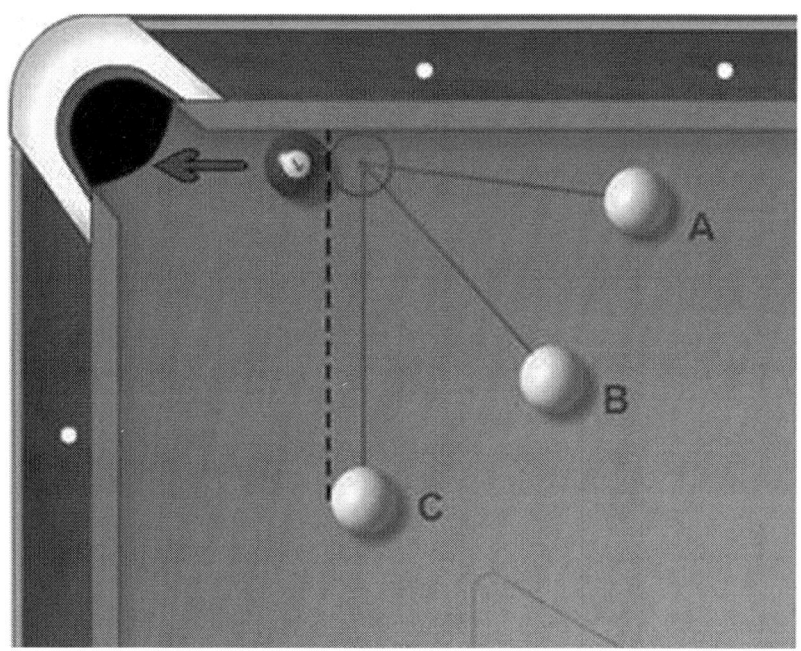

Different positions of the cue ball require different angles of collision

Adding Some Spin – spinning the ball correctly is certainly an advantage over any opponent because it enables you to setup your next shot, pull off shots that seem impossible with no spin, and make the opponent's move more difficult.

Learning how to spin the ball is not so complicated but mastering it is quite difficult and even professional players sometimes struggle with side spins. Spins can be separated according to the area of the ball you intend to hit and they are called a top spin, back spin, and side spins (left and right).

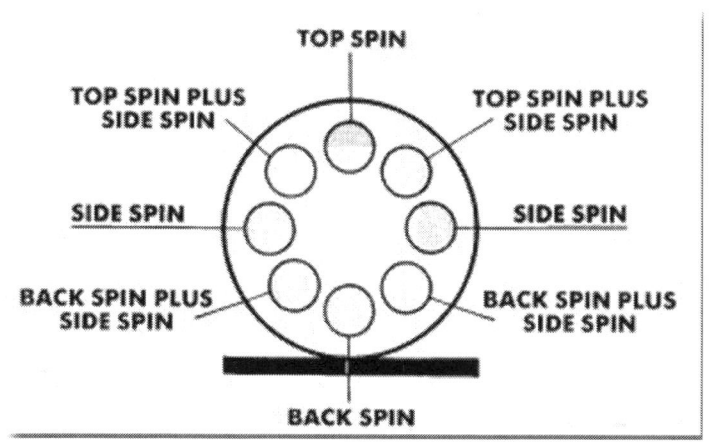

Different spins and positions on the cue ball needed to achieve it

The top spin is used if you want the cue ball to continue traveling forward even after the contact with the target ball. This is useful if you want to set up your next shot after making the first one, especially if your other balls are on the other end of the table. Raise your non-shooting hand in order to be more accurate and avoid situations where you simply miss the ball or hit it too lightly.

The back spin is useful for two situations: if you want the cue ball to stop as soon as it hits the target ball or if you want the cue ball to slowly return backward. If you want the cue ball to stop, try hitting it slightly below the center and below your usual shot. This takes a bit of practice but it's the easiest of all spins. On the other hand, if you want the ball to backspin, hit it even lower. This can get tricky sometimes because beginners tend to hit too low and end up making the ball jump. You can also control the backspin by hitting the ball slightly to the side.

The side spin is definitely the most difficult of all spins and mastering it takes a long time. However, it is quite a useful tool for making shots that would otherwise seem impossible, especially when your path is blocked by your opponent's balls or the 8 ball. The objective is to hit the ball either to the left or to the right while still keeping close to the center unless you want to add some topspin or backspin. This spin is used mostly when the player wants to control how the cue ball is going to reflect off the rails. For example, using the left side spin, the ball will reflect further to the left after hitting a cushion and the amount of spin depends on where you hit the ball and how strong did you do it.

Physics and Geometry behind Every Shot

Physics and mathematics of pool revolve around two or more billiard balls colliding. The pool table is not a perfect system since there is some friction between the balls and the table's surface but the friction force is not great enough to cause trouble as it can only slow the balls insignificantly without changing their direction.

Pool balls are also generally quite smooth and they have the same mass, making these predictions almost 100% accurate.

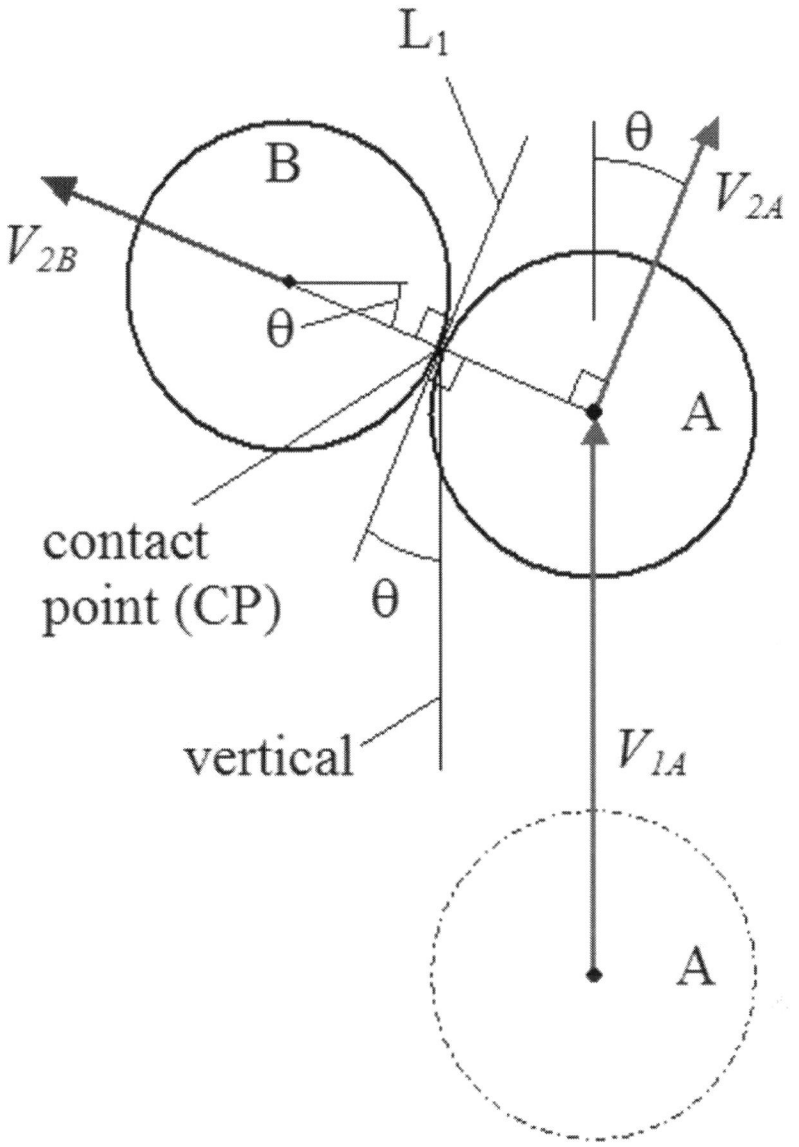

As we can see in the figure, when the ball A hits the ball B, its velocity changes from V_{1A} to V_{2A}. The B ball is initially at rest and its final speed is denoted as V_{2B}. The angle θ shows up at several places. It's the angle showing the difference between the original direction of the ball A and the direction it gets after the impact. Due to L_1 being tangent to the contact point (CP), the angle between L_1 and the vertical is also θ. Finally, the angle between the horizontal (line perpendicular to the vertical and the original path of ball A) and the line connecting the centers of two balls is also θ. This figure lets us conclude that the B ball will move in the direction of the line which connects two centers. This line is perpendicular to the tangent line and this assumption checks out because the force of the ball A is delivered perpendicularly to the ball B. Apart from being able to guess the direction of ball B, we can also assume that the A ball is going to deflect perpendicularly to the direction of ball B's movement and here is the proof.

Two billiard balls colliding is an example of energy and momentum conservation. This means that the momentum and the kinetic energy of the system before and after the collision must remain the same. In the beginning, only the ball A is moving and possessing momentum and energy but after the collision, both ball A and ball B are moving, leading us to this equation.

$$m_A \times V_{1A} = m_A \times V_{2A} + m_B \times V_{2B}$$

Let's cancel out the masses because they are equal.

$$V_{1A} = V_{2A} + V_{2B}$$

It's obvious to see that all of the momentum is transferred. Let's see how the kinetic energy of this system behaves.

$$\frac{1}{2}m_A \times (V_{1A})^2 = \frac{1}{2}m_A \times (V_{2A})^2 + \frac{1}{2}m_B \times (V_{2B})^2$$

Since the masses are the same we can cancel them out, as well as the ½ fraction.

$$(V_{1A})^2 = (V_{2A})^2 + (V_{2B})^2$$

Since these velocities are vector quantities, we can represent them using vector lines. However, the equation tells us that we are dealing with a right-angled triangle since the square of one side (the hypotenuse) is equal to the sum of the other two sides (catheti). Let's draw that triangle.

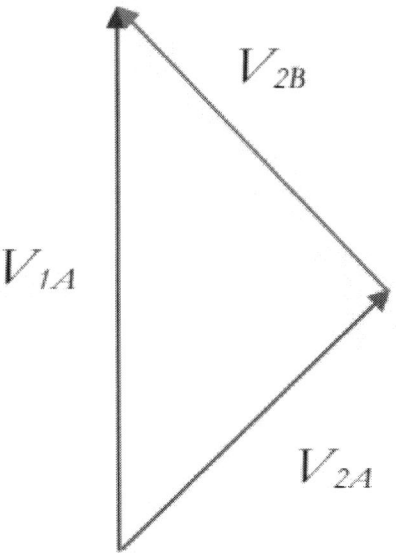

This shows us that the cue ball and our object ball will always move perpendicular to each other after collision. In order to take advantage of this, point your index finger in line with the desired path of the target ball and stretch out your thumb to make a right angle with the index. The direction your thumb is showing is the path of the cue ball after collision.

Planning Ahead – Strategy

A proper game of pool consists of many different things you need to stay aware of if you want to keep up with your opponent. Every single mistake can a lot in the long run because pool games, especially the ones played by beginners, can be decided in just one move. For example, if your opponent has pocketed all of his target balls and he only has the black 8 ball to pocket, you will need to carefully plan out each of your moves before you make a shot. Leaving your opponent with a clear shot after you fail to keep your turn is a big mistake and every player is sure to punish that. You will sometimes even have to focus on making it harder for your opponent rather than pocketing the last ball for yourself. There are several tips and tricks you should never forget when it comes to the game of pool. Let's take a look at the most important tips and strategies which will help you win most of your games!

- Don't hit the balls too hard! Hitting the balls too hard is bad from a lot of different perspectives. First of all, even if you succeed to make an accurate shot, a lot of unprofessional pool tables may simply cause the ball to fall out of the pocket, even though it went in for a millisecond. Additionally, this may cause you to miss the shots originally destined to pocket because they hit the nearby cushion too hard and reflected off the pocket. A light shot would have probably caused the ball to hit the cushion but it wouldn't reflect so hard and it would still go in. Finally, it doesn't matter if your shot is precise or not, hitting the ball lightly will ensure that the target ball remains close to the pocket even if you miss the shot.

- Try to pocket balls clustered together early in the game. After the break shot, there is going to be a lot of balls stuck to each other which means you might end up in a situation where a lot of your target balls are clustered together near the pocket. Pocketing all of them requires a lot of thinking because a single misjudged shot may disrupt their order and you might end up only pocketing one of them and feeling regretful about not pocketing them all. You need to play close attention to where your cue ball is going to end and you will often have to apply backspin to ensure the cue ball returns after the collision.

- Take care of the center of the table first! Pocketing balls in the two middle pockets is definitely harder than putting balls in the corner pockets because the cushions protect it from both sides, limiting the angle and the margin of a successful shot. That is why your priority should be to pocket balls positioned near the center holes when the cue ball is also near the center. Be extra careful when trying to get the perfect shot for the middle pockets since a slight inaccuracy can cause you to miss the shot. Also, try light shots for the middle pockets since balls tend to fall out from it.

Hitting balls with power can cause them to enter the pocket and exit immediately.

- Plan ahead. Pocketing a ball should be just one of the goals of your every move because your next move in the same inning may turn out to be awful if you don't plan ahead. However, if you do and if you try to predict where the cue ball is going to end up, you can set yourself up for a series of successful shots without letting your opponent take control. If you end up in an impossible situation where you can't pocket any of your object balls, try to leave the cue ball in a position where your opponent simply won't have any options but to return the inning to you. Stay careful and try not to commit a foul doing so.

- Keep things simple. If you are a beginner and if you have already played several matches, possibly winning some of them, you are probably still under prepared for difficult shots which even the pool professionals struggle with. That is why it's always better to settle for simple shots and playing it safe rather than going for a shot which has a low chance of success. It's better to use your turn to set up your next move than to try an impossible shot and leave your opponent with a clear path.

- Try to learn from your opponent. It's always better to play against more skilled opponents because you can learn a lot just from observing. Additionally, finally beating them is going to feel great and it's going to happen sooner or later. Observe their every shot, their tactics and the way they choose which shot to take. Finally, be sure to stay aware of their weaknesses. Unless you are playing with a professional pool tournament winner, your opponent is going to show a weakness and it might be his struggle with long range shots, failing to play the ball against the cushion, etc. Exploit that weakness and try to leave him with a shot he's been struggling with the entire game.

- There are no easy shots. A lot of beginners who have mastered the basics of hitting the ball sometimes fail to hit even the simplest of shots because they don't pay enough attention. Focus on every shot with the same amount of concentration because you simply can't afford to miss the clear shot in a game of pool.

How to Amaze Your Friends?

After you master the basics and after you end up winning several matches and hitting some rather difficult shots, you might be interested in some ways which can make you appear somewhat more experienced and skilled than your opponents. Pool offers quite a large variety of different skill shots but they are often quite difficult to master. A trick shot is only successful if it ends up pocketing one of our target balls and keeping your turn. Let's take a look at several ones the most worthy of our attention.

Pocketing the 8 Ball During the Break Shot

As you probably already know, pocketing only the 8 ball during the break shot ensures an automatic victory. However, the 8 ball is in the middle of the triangle rack and it's surrounded by other balls at each side, making it difficult to even move it towards a rail, let alone pocketing it. However, there is one technique which is worth a shot if you manage to hit it correctly.

Your best bet is to place the cue ball near one of the side rails during the break shot and aim for either the right or left ball in the second row, depending on which side you chose. Stay aware of the fact that you can't hit the cue ball dead center because you will likely scratch in the bottom pocket. You need to put some spin on it. Your spin should be low right if you are breaking from the left side and vice versa. Pool players often refer to spins using the clock to refer to positions. This means you will either have to hit to ball either at 5:00 if you are shooting from the left rail and at 7:00 if you are shooting from the right rail. Aim strong and the 8 ball should go into the side pocket opposite of the rail you chose to break from. This is not an easy shot and there is no way someone can hit it with 100% accuracy. However, it is worth a shot because these are the ways to increase your chances to nail this shot.

The perfect position to pocket the 8 ball in the side pocket opposite to the player

Jump Shot

This is more than just a regular jump shot since this shot is sometimes your only valuable option, especially if your opponent's ball is blocking all of your options. A jump shot is generally easy to perform but quite difficult to keep accurate. Your cue ball needs to keep a straight direction even after landing if you want the shot to be worth the effort.

A legal jump shot sends the ball flying but it has to land on the table. Be careful not to hit the ball too hard since sending it off the table causes a foul. Additionally, be careful while hitting the ball since you are only allowed to touch it once. The illegal way of jumping the cue ball is by hitting it too low since it will cause illegal contact. The legal way of doing it is by elevating the cue stick and hitting the cue ball somewhere above the center.

If the ball you need to jump over is close to the cue ball try hitting the cue ball with the angle close to 60 degrees which will cause it to fly higher. However, if the ball you need to jump over is further away, you need to hit the ball with the angle of 30 degrees which will cause the ball to fly lower but further.

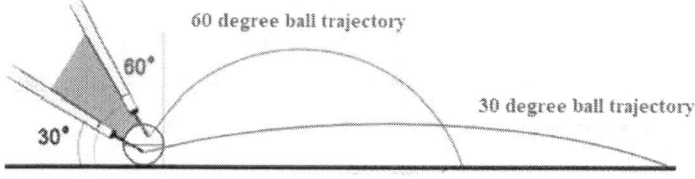

The difference between 30 and 60-degree ball trajectory

These angles are not obligatory and you will sometimes have to decide how to position your cue stick yourself. After a couple of successful jump shots, you are sure to improve it and try experimenting with different ball and cue positions. Mastering this shot is quite difficult because even a slight inaccuracy during the shot can cause the cue ball to go in a different direction than planned. A lot of beginners do an accidental jump shot when trying to do a backspin or topspin and that is something to be aware of.

4 in a Line – Trick Shot

One of the beautiful things about pool is the number of beautiful shots you can practice outside of a match. You can find a lot of instructions online about setting up for a trick shot and performing it. Doing the shot usually requires some precision and several tries but the difficult part is actually setting up and preparing the shot. The trick shot will only work if you place the target balls properly.

This trick uses four object balls lined up around the foot spot, just like in the picture. Start off by placing any ball on the foot spot. The next ball you place should be parallel to the short cushion. The second ball you place should be placed near the first ball with a slight gap between them. These are the middle balls. The outer balls should be frozen to the middle balls and both of them should face the middle pockets. The cue ball should be placed two and a half diamonds from the short rail and one diamond from the long one. A diamond is the marking on a pool table and they are usually white.

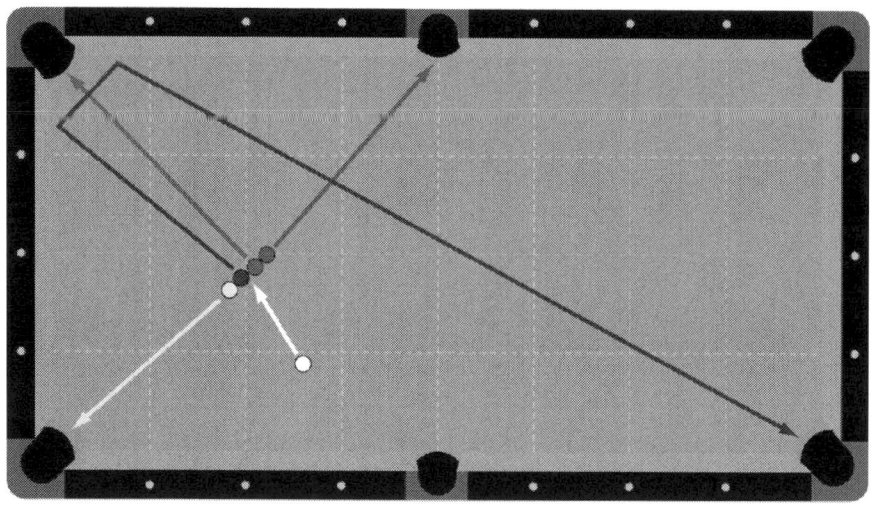

The perfect alignments of the balls required for this trick shot

After you hit the shot the balls should follow the path marked on the first figure. Trick shots like this one are quite difficult to perform because it's easy to simply align the target balls in a wrong order to fail it. However, a bit of practice makes perfect and a lot of tricks are similar in execution. After you master several of them, invite your friends and have them check your tricks out. It's guaranteed that you will need to do a lot of tutoring!

Conclusion

Playing pool for fun is quite easy since there are not a lot of rules to remember. Rules vary from country to country and from town to town since most people have adapted to their rules without consulting with the agreed upon international rules. Every single rule should be questioned before starting a match to avoid confusion and to ensure that a game is played fairly and properly. Most players start playing in bars and cafes which feature several pool tables and newcomers often have to adapt to the universal rules.

Eight-ball is definitely all about practice and strategy. People who have just started playing pool may start up great but they tend to make a lot of unforgivable mistakes which are regularly punished by their opponents in numerous ways. Pool is not just about pocketing a ball. It's about setting yourself up for many moves and not letting your opponent run the table. Keeping your turn for as long as possible is the key to winning and leaving your opponent with a clear shot can turn out to be fatal, especially if he only has the 8 ball left to pocket.

There are many other variations of pool games besides the ones we mentioned but even experienced pool players are not so familiar with them and you will rarely see any of them played professionally or in a bar. Eight-ball is definitely the most beginner friendly game of them all and every pool beginner should focus on mastering this game first. It will give you the basics of what it takes to play pool without difficult rules such as calling every shot and every hole, etc. Even though eight-ball seems fairly simple when it comes to the rule set, it is a game of strategy and planning ahead. Sometimes it's better not to try a difficult shot and leave a difficult situation for your opponent because he may end up returning the turn to you in no time.

No shot is difficult and every single one requires attention and concentration. A lot of players miss a clean shot simply because they want to show off or they don't aim properly thinking it has to go in. Always stay ahead of your every move by trying to predict the path of both your target ball and the cue ball by following the laws of physics and geometry from this book.

The most important thing about playing pool is enjoying every minute of it. There is no better way to relax than playing a game of pool with your friends since it is an interesting activity which doesn't require a lot of physical effort but it requires thinking planning, and a pinch of skill. What makes it so great is the fact that everyone can play it, even folks who are not so keen on other sports such as soccer, basketball, etc. Just pick up a cue stick, aim properly and you will find that seeing your target ball roll in a pocket is one of the best feelings you can experience!

If you enjoyed this book as much as I've enjoyed writing it, you can subscribe* to my email list for exclusive content and sneak peaks of my future books.

Click the link below:
http://eepurl.com/dvdExn

OR

Use the QR Code:

(*Must be 13 years or older to subscribe)

Printed in Great Britain
by Amazon